You're NEW FAVORITE

book was made possible with the help of

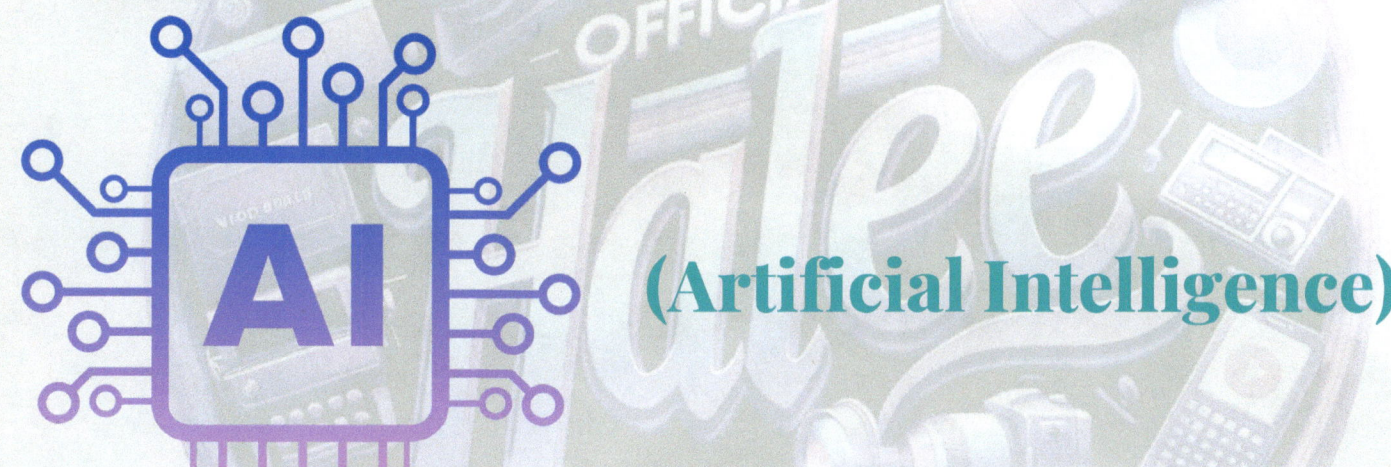

AI (Artificial Intelligence)

100% of all writing is completed by Officially Halee. This book does not contain any text generated from AI, only images.

Teen author Officially Halee has been writing since she was seven years old. As a child, Officially Halee wanted her stories published, but lacked industry resources such as a publisher and illustrator. Now a teenager, Officially Halee is equipped with better resources, including AI. Officially Halee used her descriptive writing skills to prompt AI to create illustrations for this book.

HUMAN WRITING SKILLS ➕ 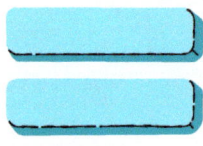 IMAGES 🟰 A GREAT BOOK

Take the Pledge!

 I will respect food allergy kids.

 I will not bully food allergy kids.

 I will speak up for food allergy kids.

Officially Published LLC

www.officiallyhalee.com

Copyright @ 2025 Officially Halee

All rights reserved. No part of this book may be reproduced, distributed, or transmitted, in any form by any means, including photocopying, recording, or any other electronic methods without prior written permission of the copyright owner, except the use of brief quotations in a book review.

To request permissions, contact the publisher at:
info@officiallypublished.com

ISBN: 9798990956889

Illustrations: AI generated with prompts written by Officially Halee.

FOR

all the kids who wish their families, friends, classmates, teachers and the world would take precautions and understand the seriousness of their food allergy(s).

"I can't wait for the first day of school!" Said Anna as she jumped in her bed.

"Me either! We're going to make so many new friends." Anthony shouted from across the hallway.

"We're going to be the coolest kids in the whole 2nd grade!" Anna cheered.

"Is that excitement I hear?" Mother appeared in the hallway overlooking the twins' rooms.

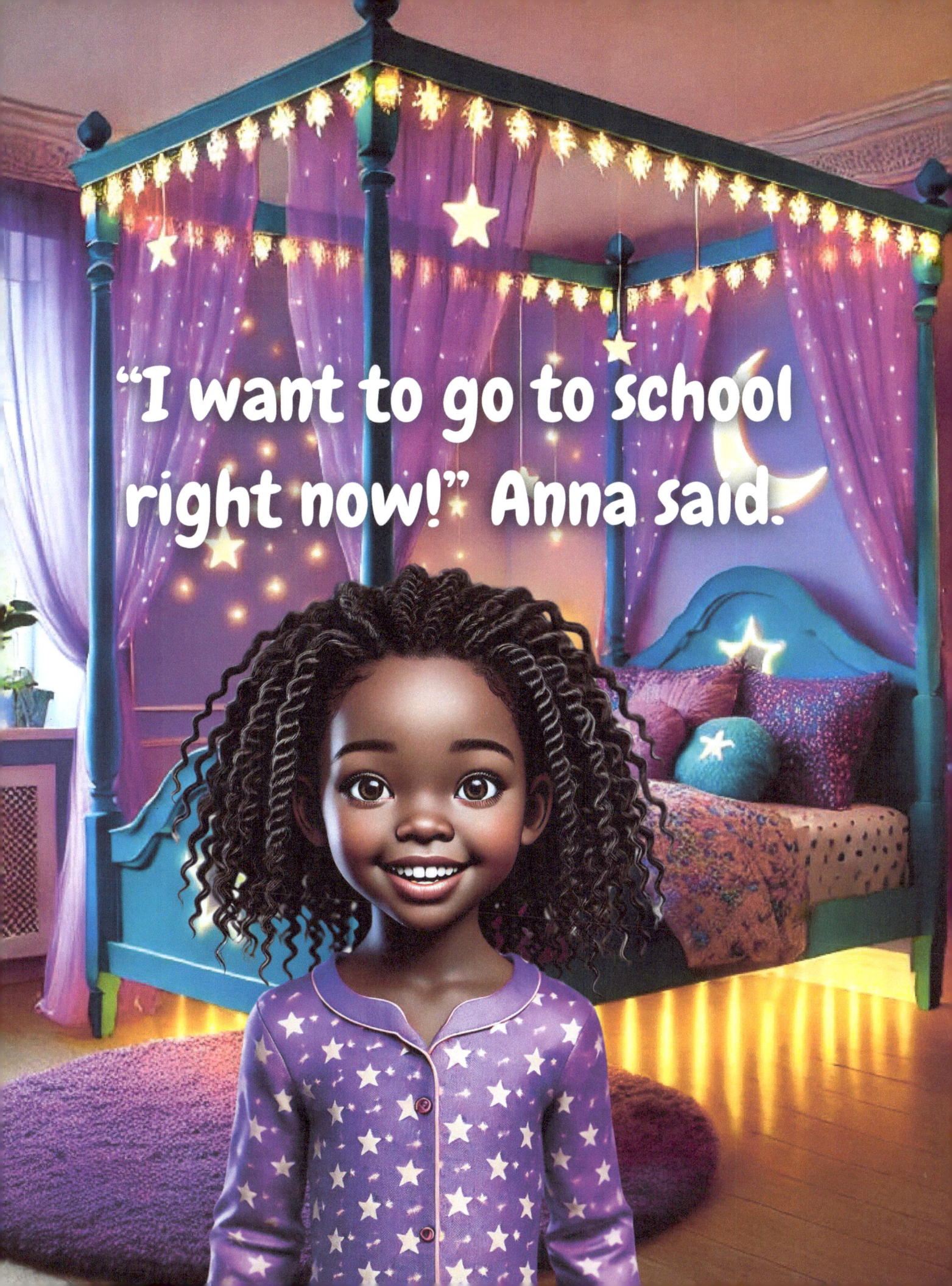

"You kids are funny. Your dad and I are happy for you, but we want to have an important talk with you both tomorrow morning before school. We love you, sweet dreams."

Sweet Dreams

"Sweet Dreams" the twins shouted back, echoing love throughout the house.

"Good Morning!" Dad greeted, smiling wide with pancakes on display.

"Good morning dad! What flavor are the pancakes?" Anthony asked as he rubbed his eyes tiredly.

"I slept great! I dreamed of slides and monkey bars! I am going to be the best in the class, I just know it!" Anna was giddy in her seat, pouring miles of syrup on her plate.

"Whoa there! Not too much syrup, Anna!" Dad warned as Anna smiled.

"How do you have this much energy? My brain is still missing my pillow." Anthony questioned.

"You have to wake up early to be a cool school kid," Mom chimed in.

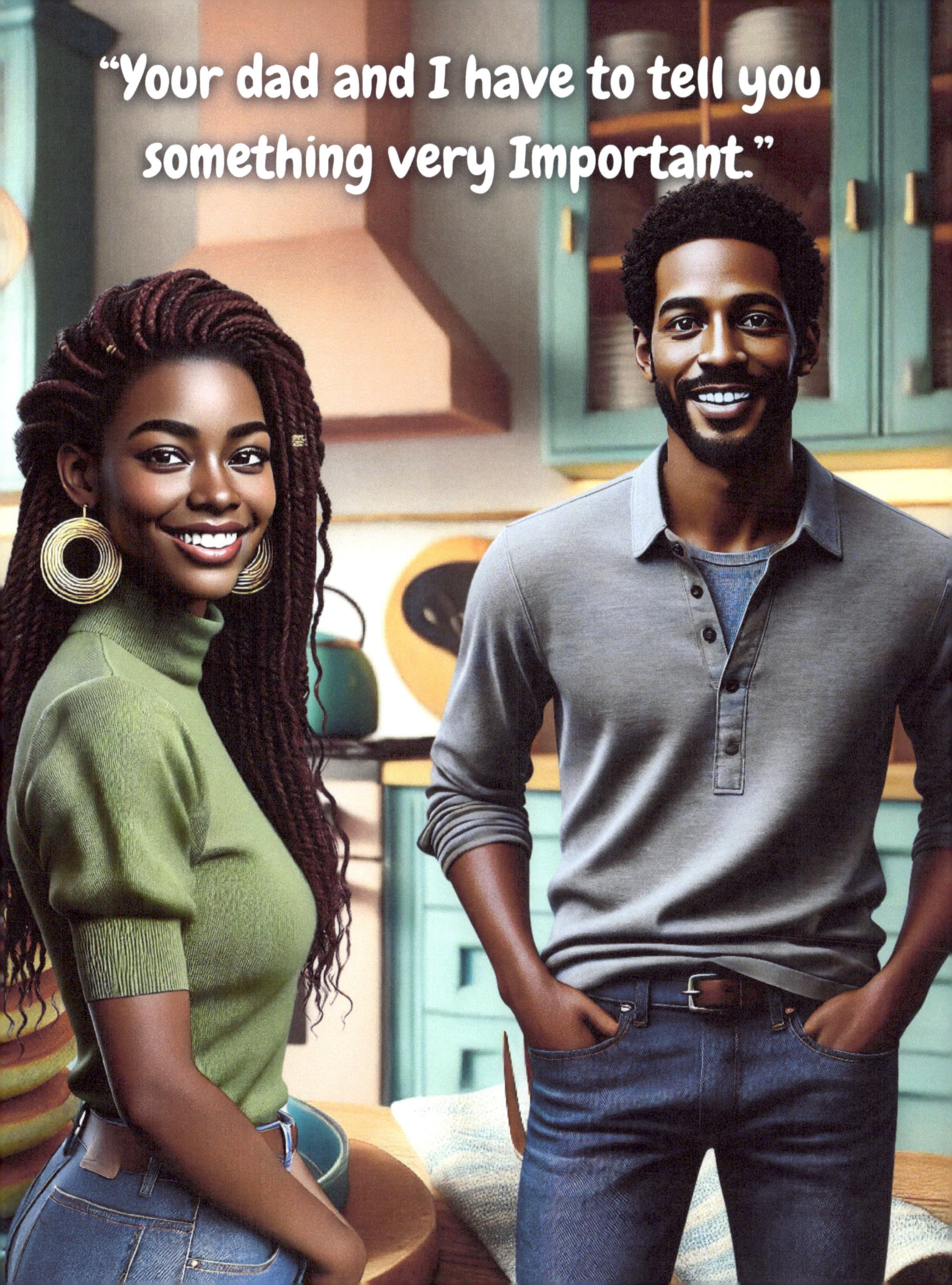

"Oh, cause we have food allergies. That makes sense" Anthony said.

"This is not a laughing matter, Anna! Taking care of yourself is important, especially when you have a food allergy." Dad said.

"I understand, but how can I take care of myself?" Anna asked.

"Very good Anna. You should wash your hands for thirty seconds at a time."

"If a food is around, always ask the teacher if your mother and I have approved it. Unfortunately, not everybody knows about your food allergy, so not all foods are safe."

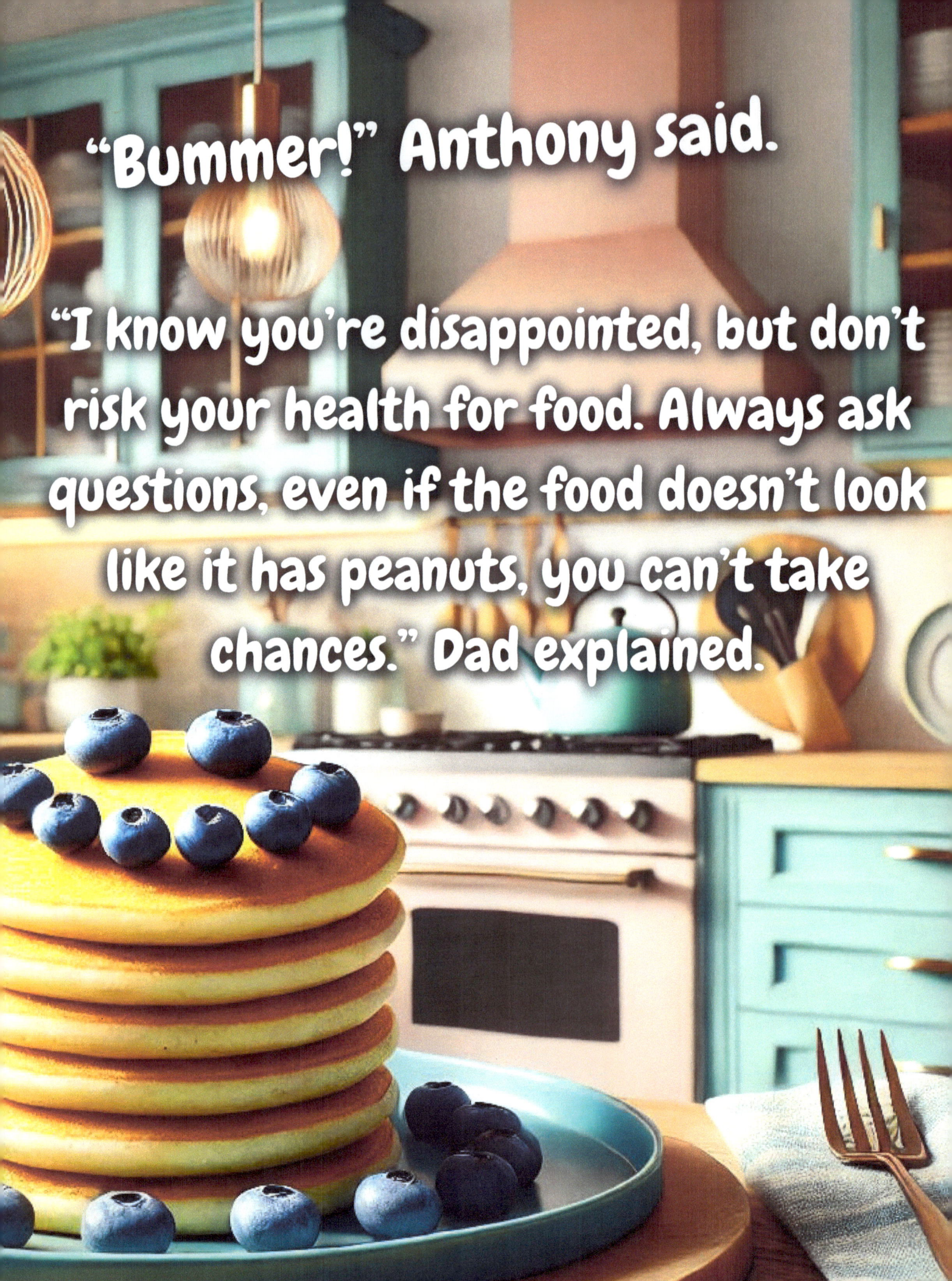

"Bummer!" Anthony said.

"I know you're disappointed, but don't risk your health for food. Always ask questions, even if the food doesn't look like it has peanuts, you can't take chances." Dad explained.

"Which brings us to another point: cross contamination. Just like your dad said, even food that does not have peanuts could have been cooked in the same kitchen as a peanut related food." Mom explained.

"How do we know if we ate something that is bad for us?" Anna asked.

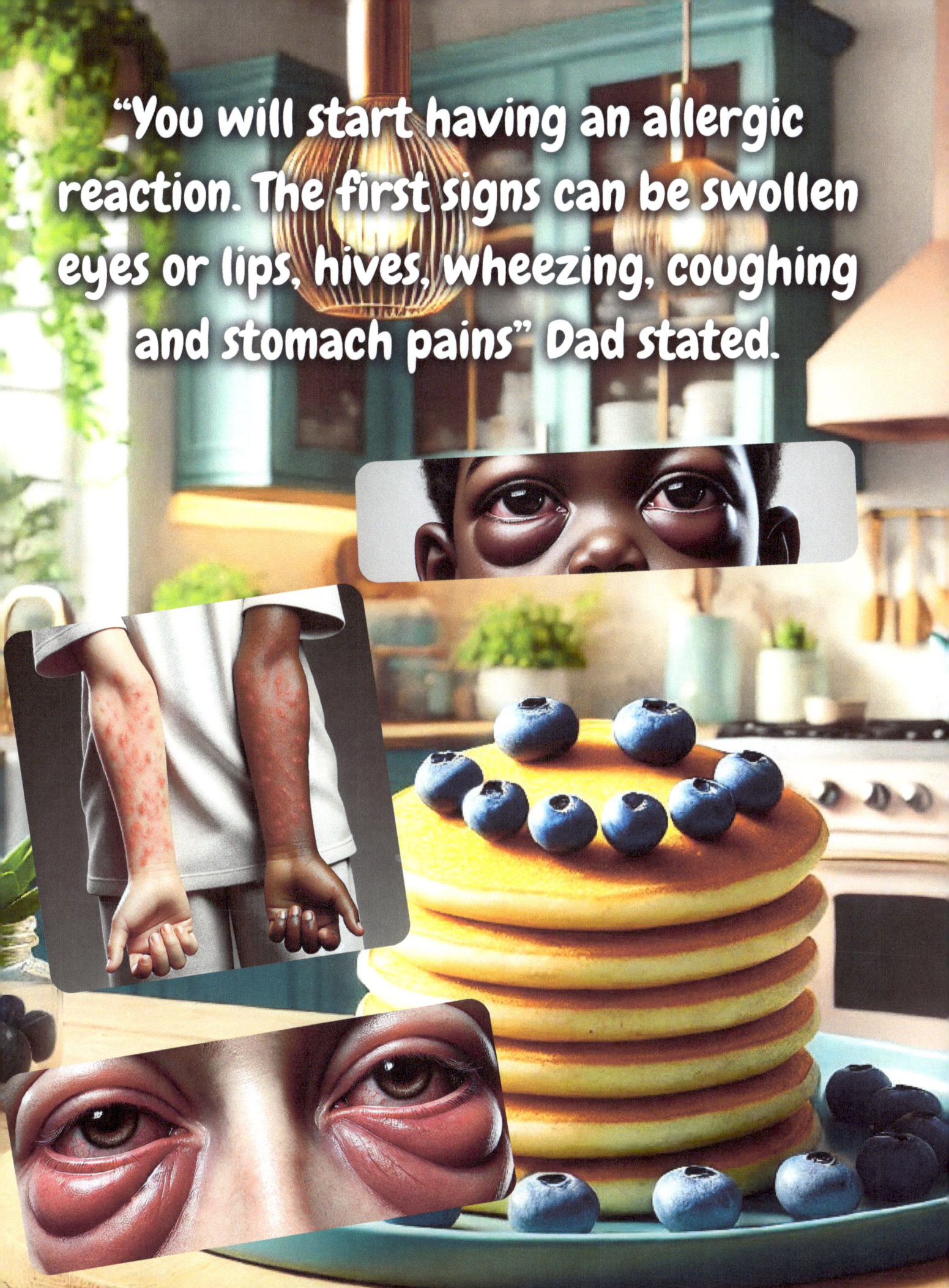

"I know a really bad allergic reaction can lead to anaphylaxis." Anna said.

"It can cause us to die." Anthony stated.

"We're glad you understand how dangerous your peanut allergy can become." Mom said.

"I'm worried. What if kids don't think I'm cool because of my food allergy?" Anthony asked from the back seat of the car.

"What if they think we're weirdos?" Anna questioned.

"Being yourself and do what it best for you. Never risk your health to be cool. The kids who understand your food allergy and respect the choices you have to make are your real friends." Dad said.

"Well said. Remember kids, if you ever feel uncomfortable or unsafe tell the teacher to call us." Mom said.

"Are you ready for your first day of 2nd grade?" Dad said.

"Anna and Anthony have a severe peanut allergy which means they can't eat or touch foods or products, that are not reviewed by their parents." Mrs. Banana explained.

"When products don't contain peanuts are made or stored in the same location as products which contain peanuts, it's called cross contamination. Cross contamination situations can cause the twins to have a food allergy reaction." Mrs. Banana continued explaining to the class.

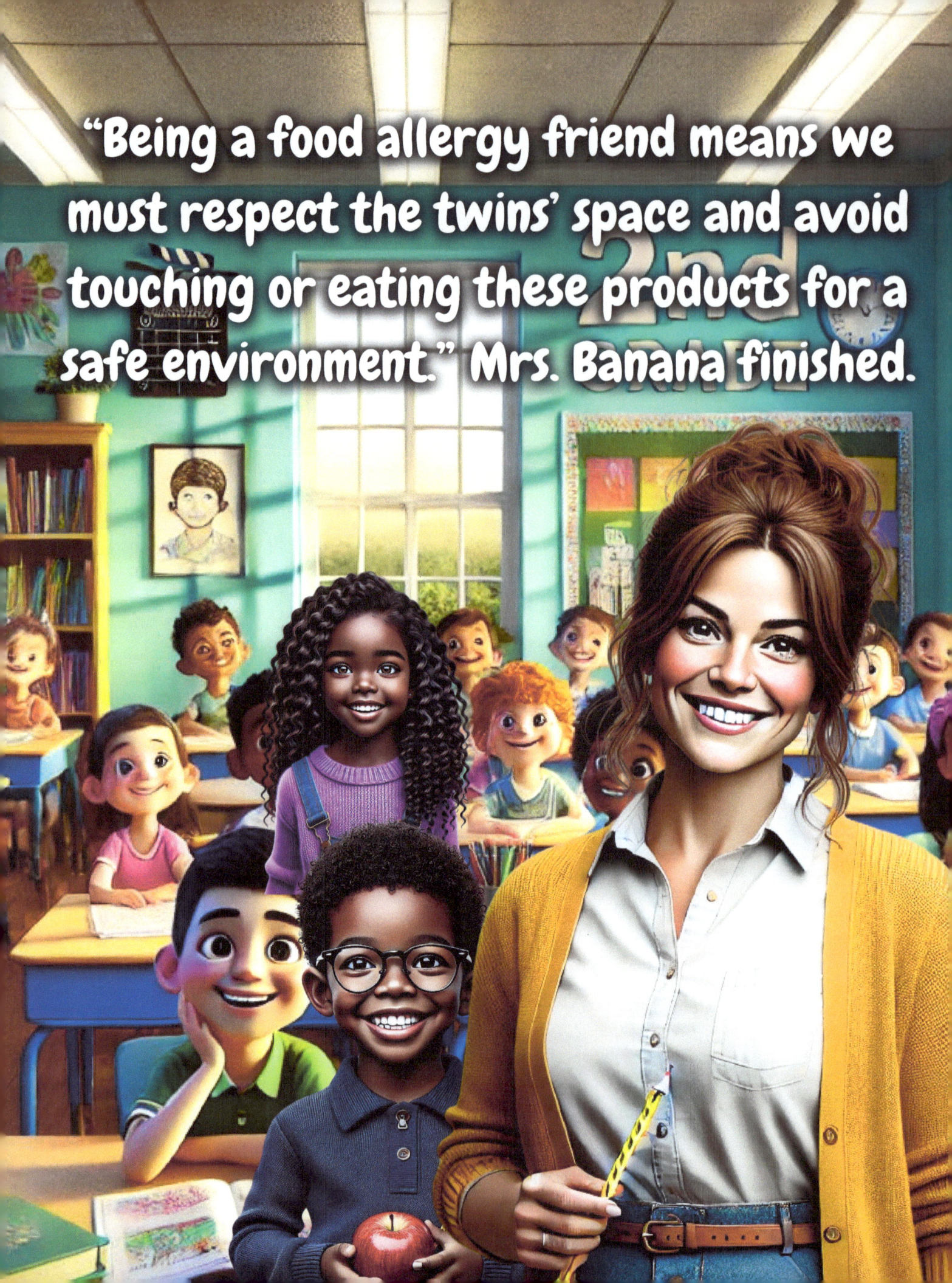

"Being a food allergy friend means we must respect the twins' space and avoid touching or eating these products for a safe environment." Mrs. Banana finished.

"I've read about you! You're so cool!" Anthony exclaimed.

"Are you going to tell the class about our food allergy?" Anna asked.

"I sure am!" Allergy Aubree said.

"Class, your new friends Anna and Anthony have a peanut allergy. A peanut allergy is when the body thinks peanut proteins are harmful. If Anna or Anthony come in contact with peanuts, they could have an allergic reaction." Allergy Aubree explained.

"Twins do you know what an allergic reaction is?" Allergy Aubree asked.

"An allergic reaction is how the body responds when my brother or I are exposed to peanuts. It can cause us to have hives, swollen eyes or lips, wheezing or stomach pains." Anna answered.

"Very good, Anna. We must respect their food allergy because it can become deadly. Here is a list of precautions and safe measures we all should be aware of:"

- Remember the signs of Anaphylaxis: swollen eyes and/or lips, difficulty breathing, wheezing, stomach pains

- Remember, always wash your hands with soap and water for 30 seconds

- Remember, to have your teacher or an adult wipe down your desk if needed

Not all signs of anapjylaxis are listed. For a full list, contact a medical professional.

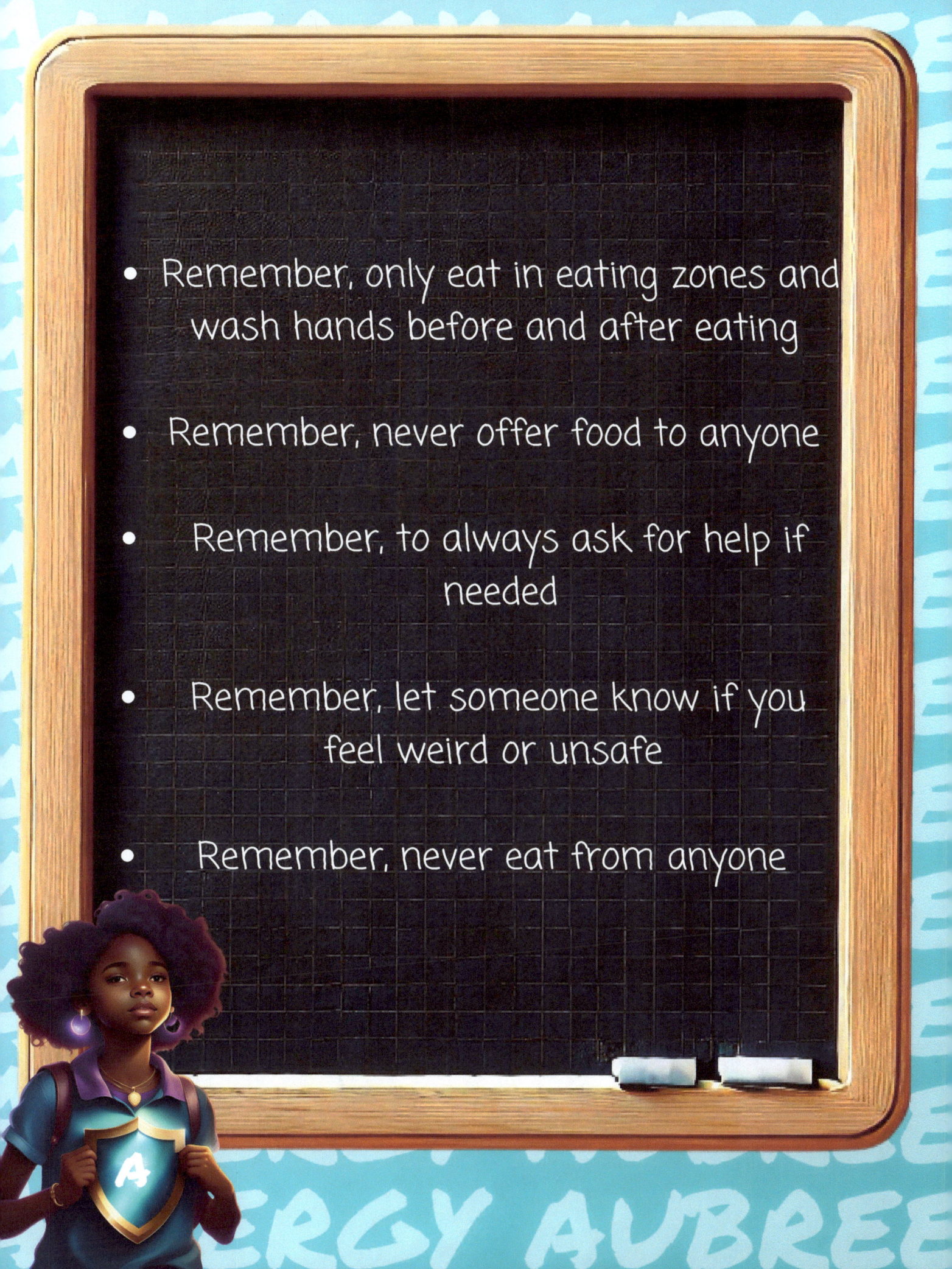

- Remember, only eat in eating zones and wash hands before and after eating

- Remember, never offer food to anyone

- Remember, to always ask for help if needed

- Remember, let someone know if you feel weird or unsafe

- Remember, never eat from anyone

- Remember, never be afraid to speak up for yourself because your safety always comes first

- Remember, food allergy kids can't eat foods that haven't been reviewed by their parents

- Remember, everyone wants to be included in fun activities so always make the environment safe for all friends

- Remember, touching can be considered cross contamination which means Anna and Anthony can't shake your hand, hug you, or eat your treats because it could harm them

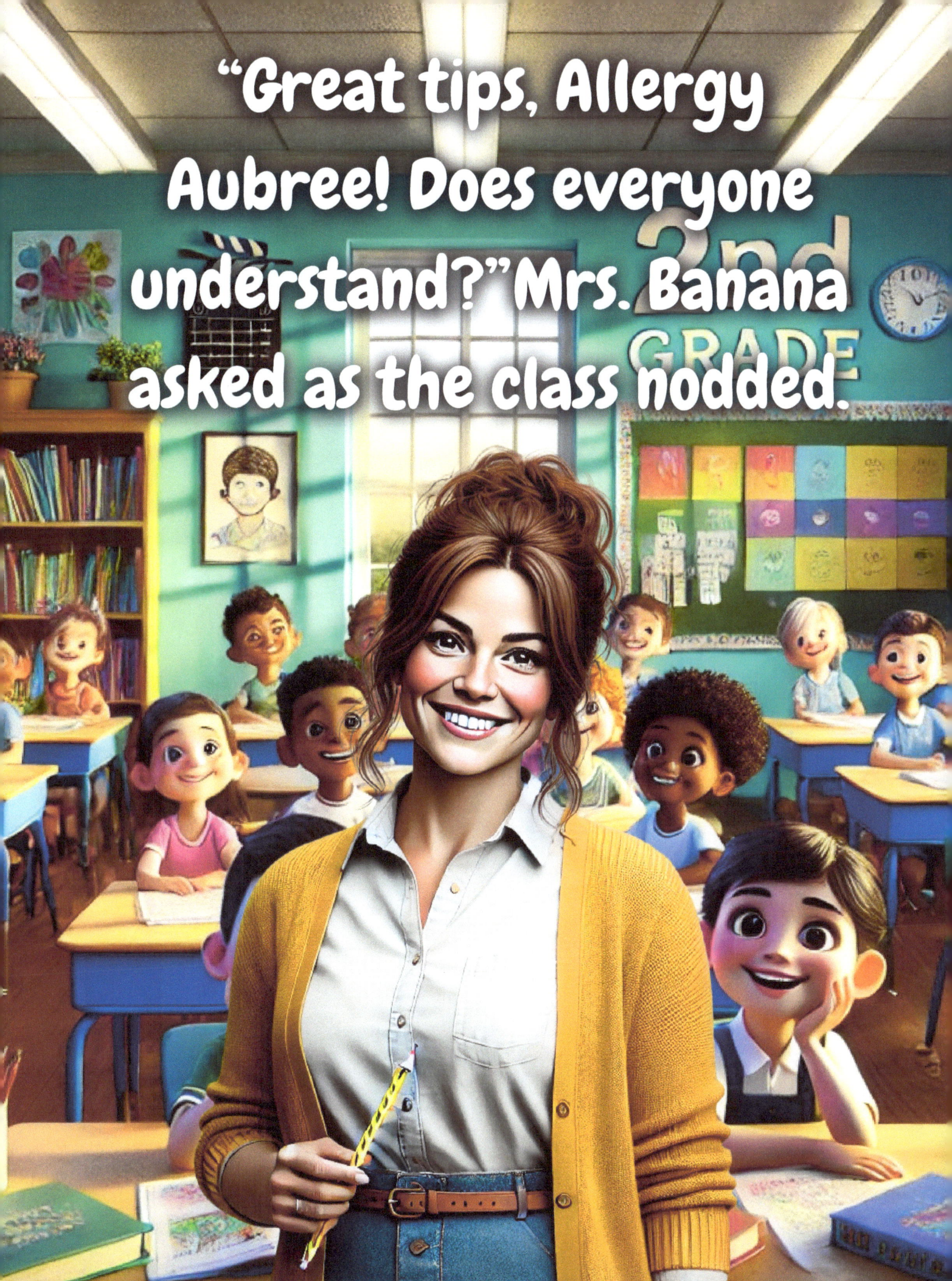

"Thanks, Ma'am. On your desk, you will find a food label take home sheet that explains how to read food labels and a list of approved foods the twins can eat. A detailed guide will be provided to your parents and teacher. Mrs. Banana will also explain the school's Food Allergy Action Plan. We want to keep our friends safe at all times." Allergy Aubree explained.

To learn about the Food Allergy Action Plan, scan the QR Code

"Thanks, Allergy Aubree! How did everyone get a sheet?" Anna asked.

"My food allergy magic! In fact, I have a food allergy, too! I am allergic to peanuts and tree nuts." Allergy Aubree answered.

"Really? Thanks for explaining our food allergy to our new class." Anthony said.

"You're welcome, twins! Have a great school year!" Allergy Aubree replied.